# TODDLER COLORING BOOK ANIMALS

# Monkey

# TODDLER

## COLORING BOOK ANIMALS

by The Coloring Book Art Design Studio

# TODDLER
## COLORING BOOK ANIMALS

# THIS BOOK

## BELONG TO

_______________________

_______________________

# LET'S TEST YOUR COLOR

# Aligator

Alpaca

Ant

# Antelope

# Armadillo

Bat

Bear

# Beaver

# Bee

# Beetle

# Buffalo

Bug

# Butterfly

Camel

Cat

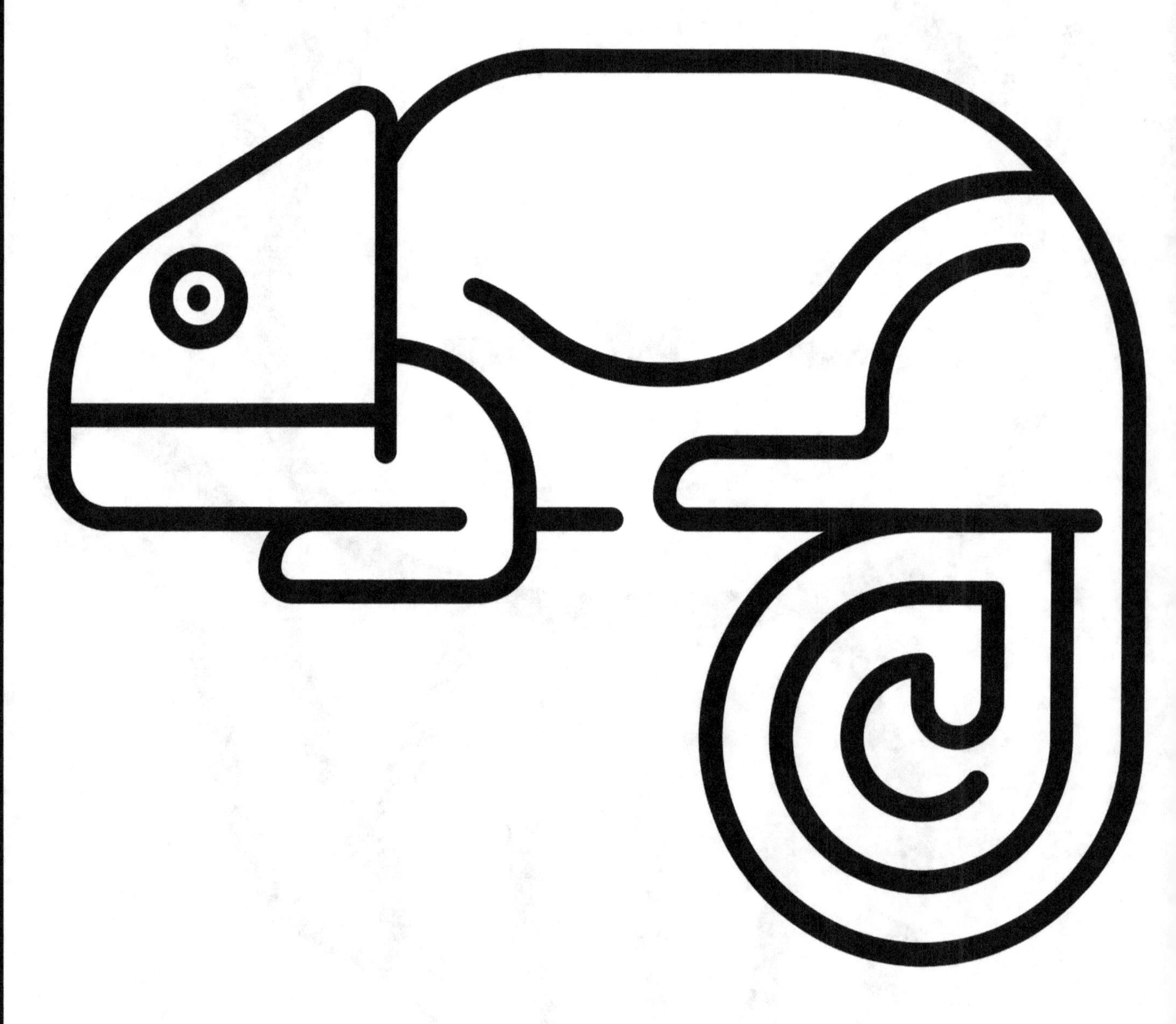

# Chameleon

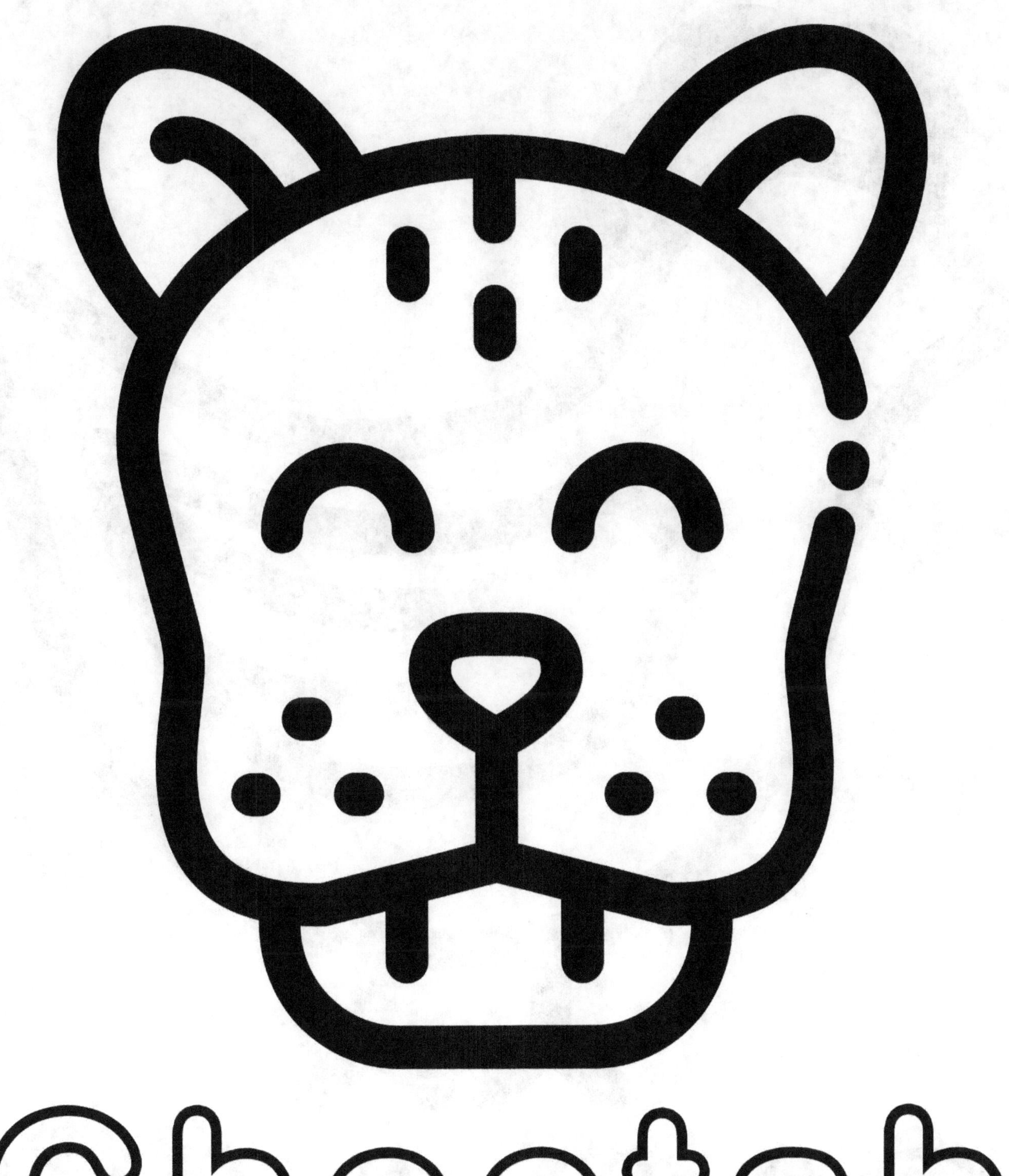

# Cheetah

# Chicken

Clam

# Clownfish

Cobra

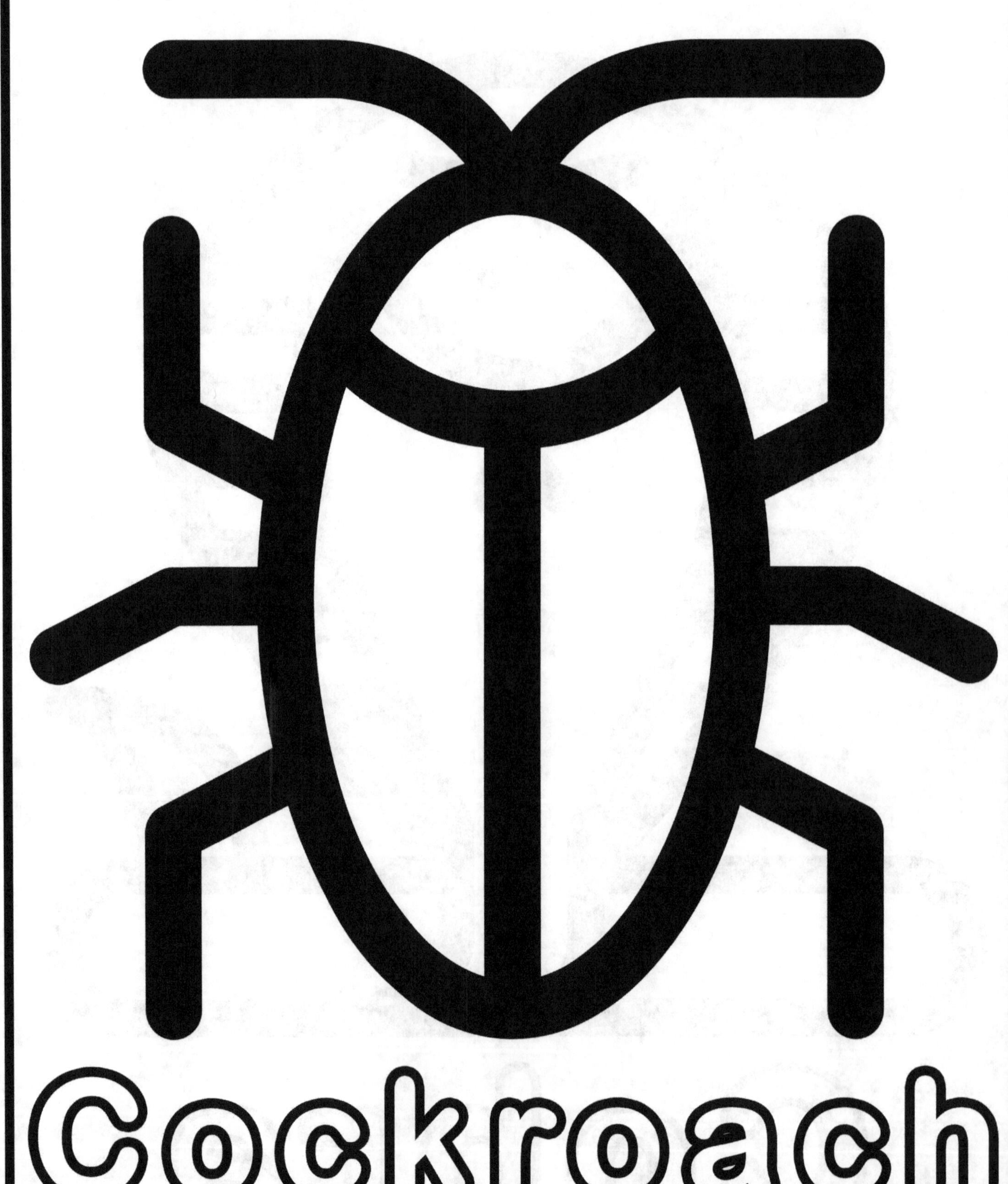

Cockroach

Cow

Crab

Crow

Deer

# Dinosaur

Dog

Dolphin

Dove

# Dragon

# Dragonfly

Duck

Eagle

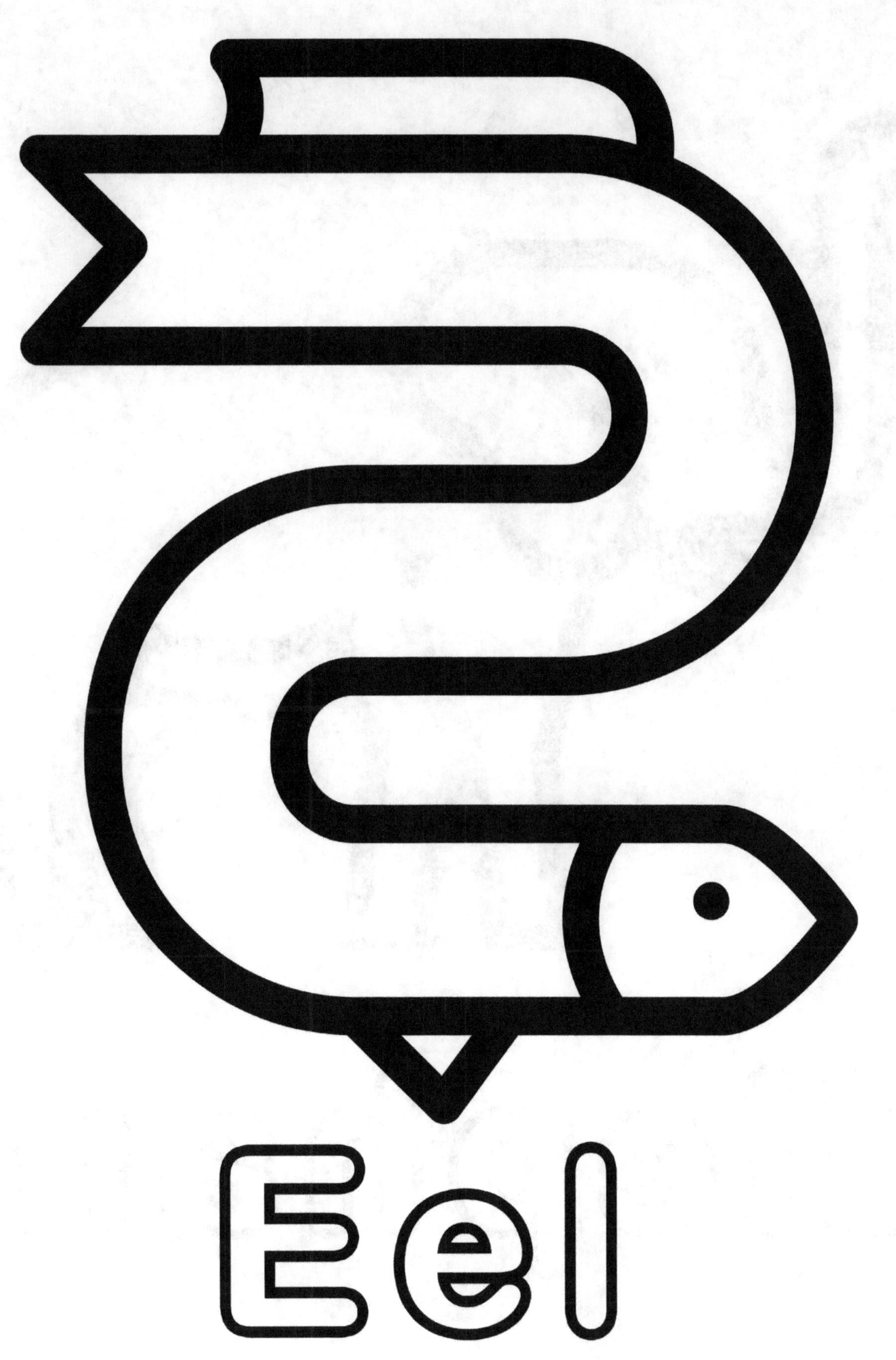

Eel

Elephant

# Fish

# Flamingo

Fox

Frog

Giraffe

Goat

Gorilla

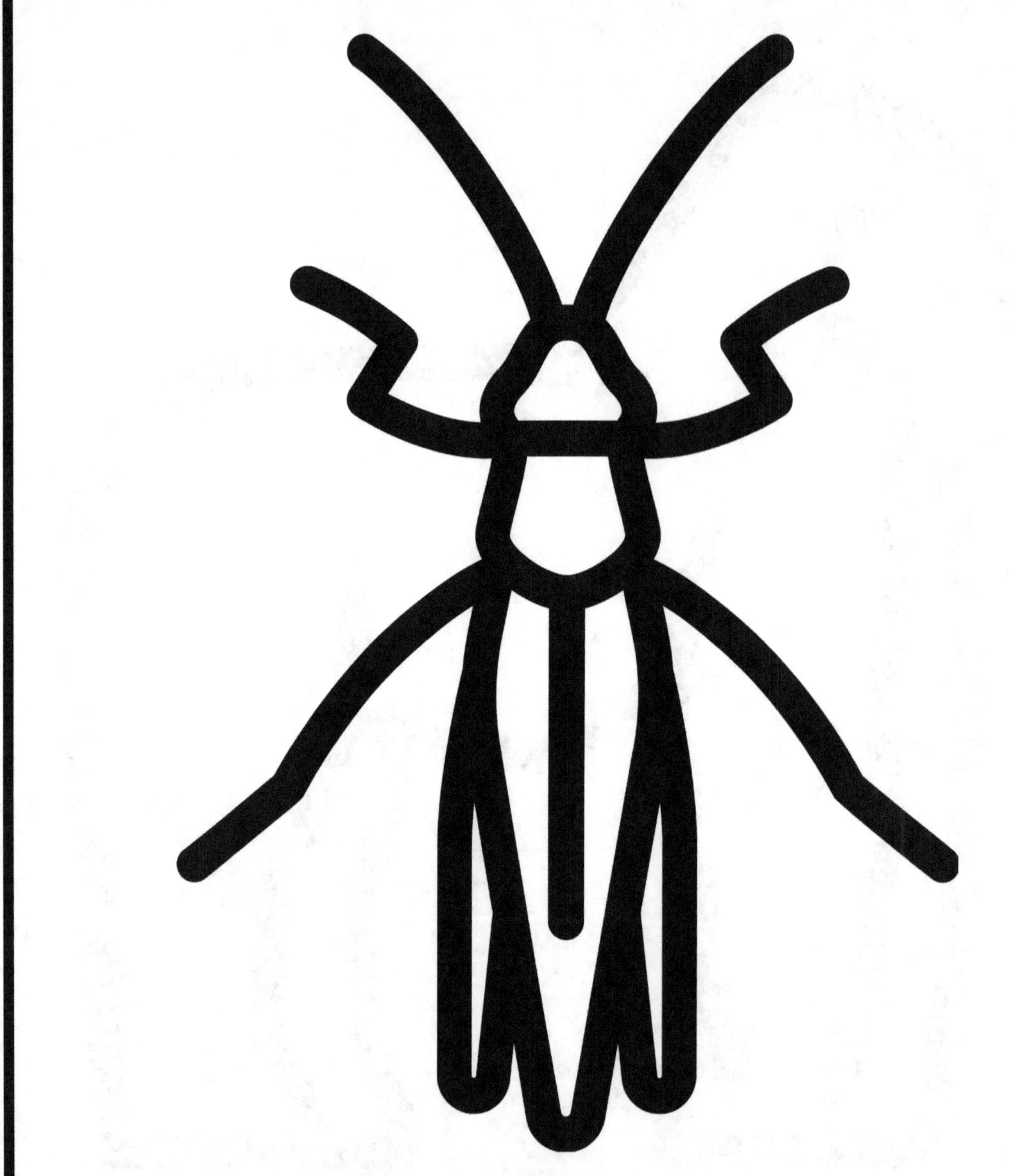

# Grasshopper

# Hamster

# Hedgehog

Hippopotamus

Horse

Jelllyfish

# Kangaroo

# Koala

# Ladybug

Leopard

Lion

Lobster

# Macaw

# Mite

Mole

Monkey

Moose

# Mosquito

Octopus

Ostrich

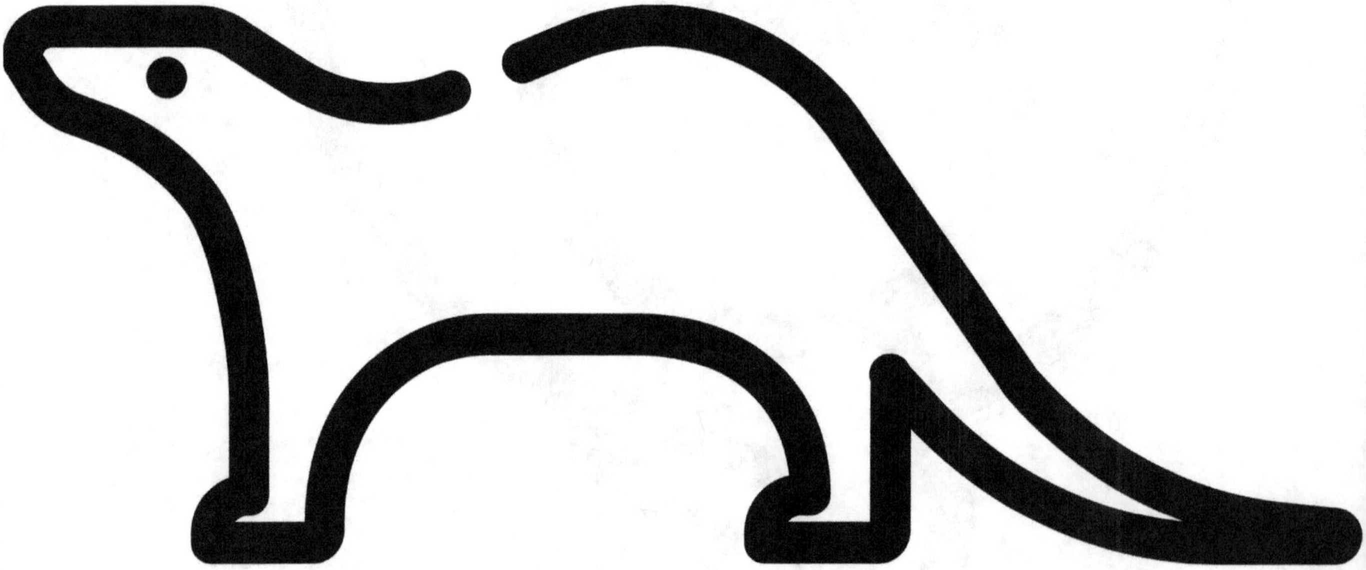

# Otter

Owl

# Oyster

Panda

# Parrot

# Peacock

# Penguin

Pig

# Platypus

# Pufferfish

Rabbit

# Raccoon

# Rat

Rhino

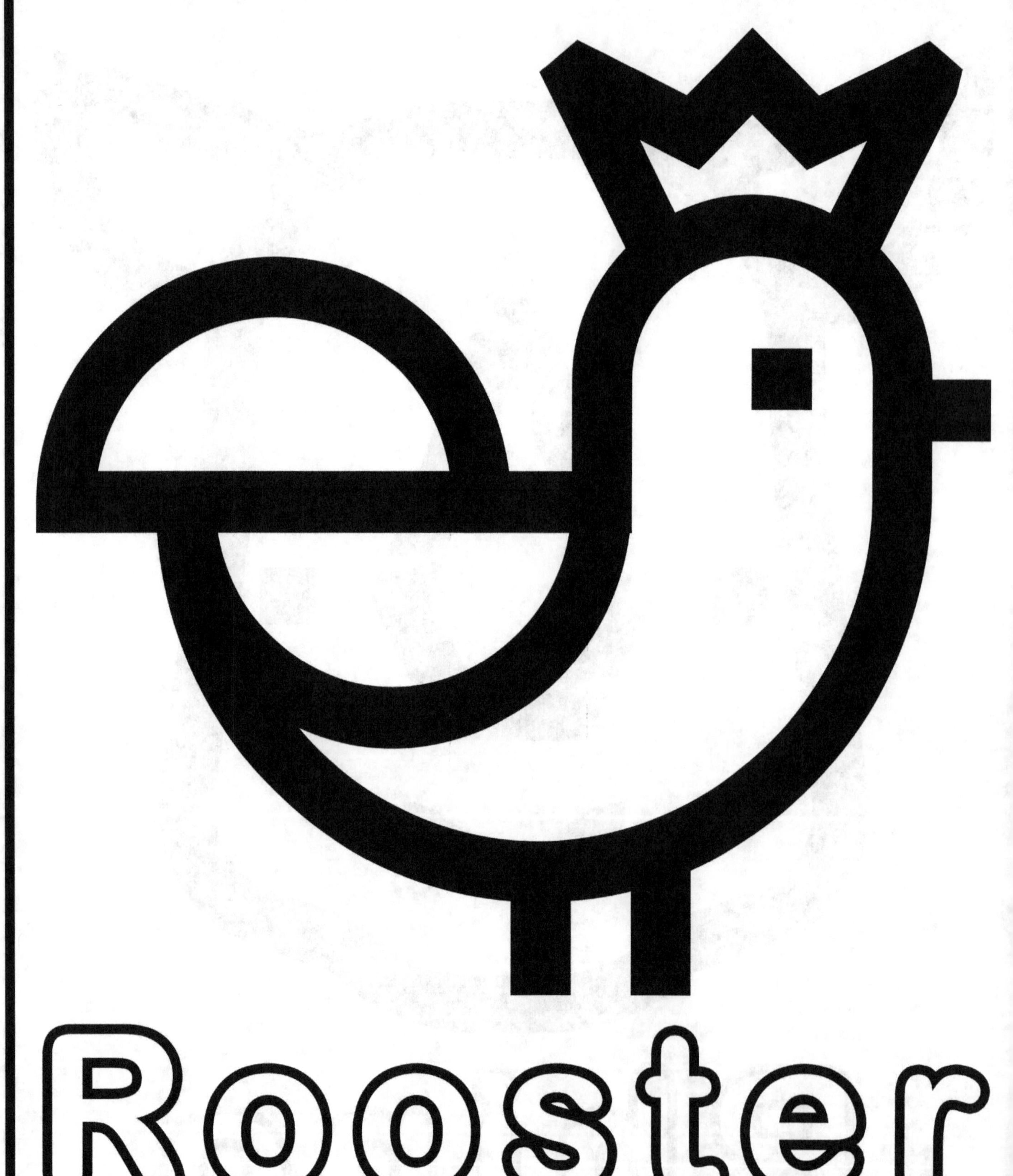

# Rooster

Scarab

# Scorpion

Sea Lion

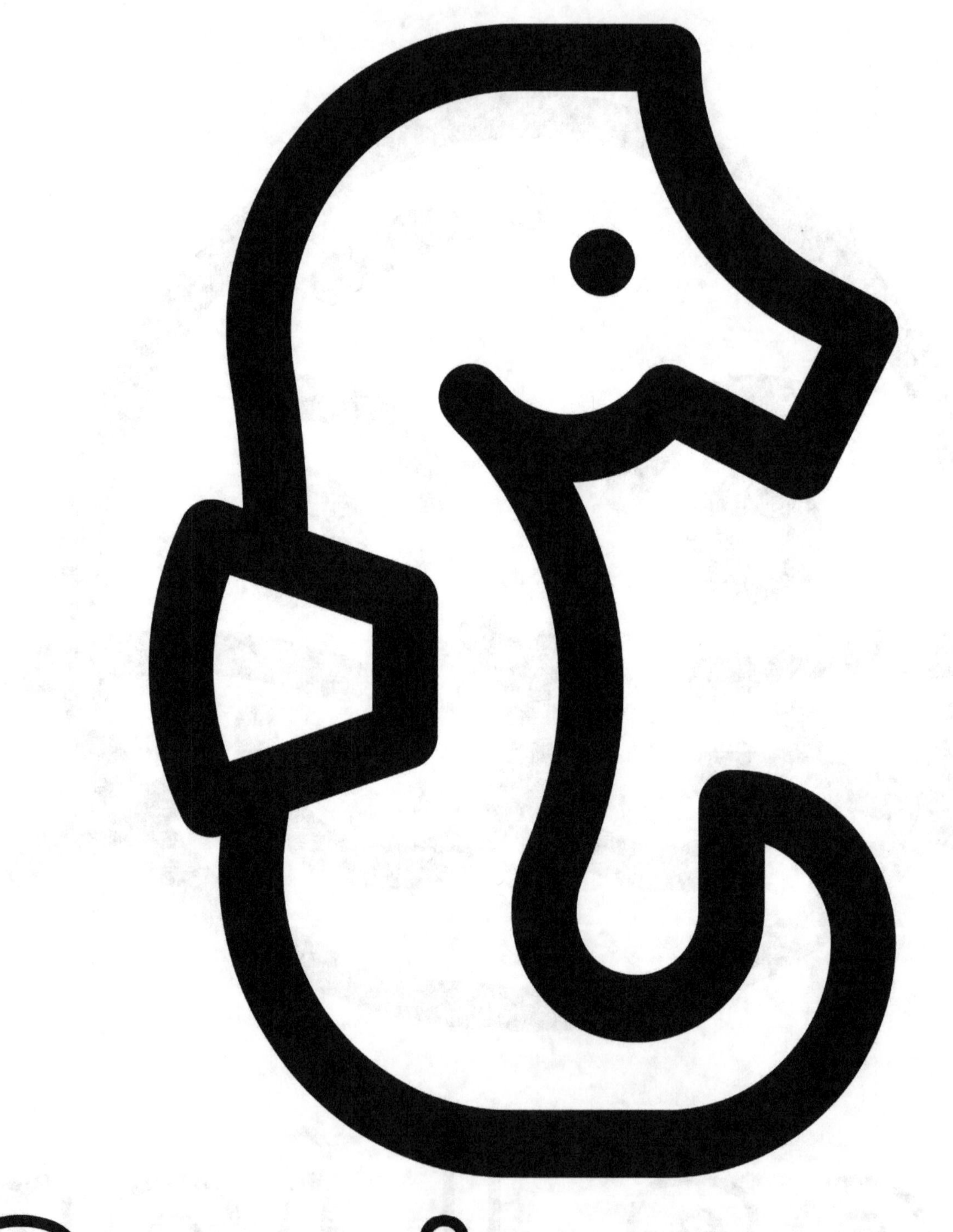

Seahorse

Shark

# Sheep

# Shrimp

Skunk

Sloth

Snail

Snake

Spider

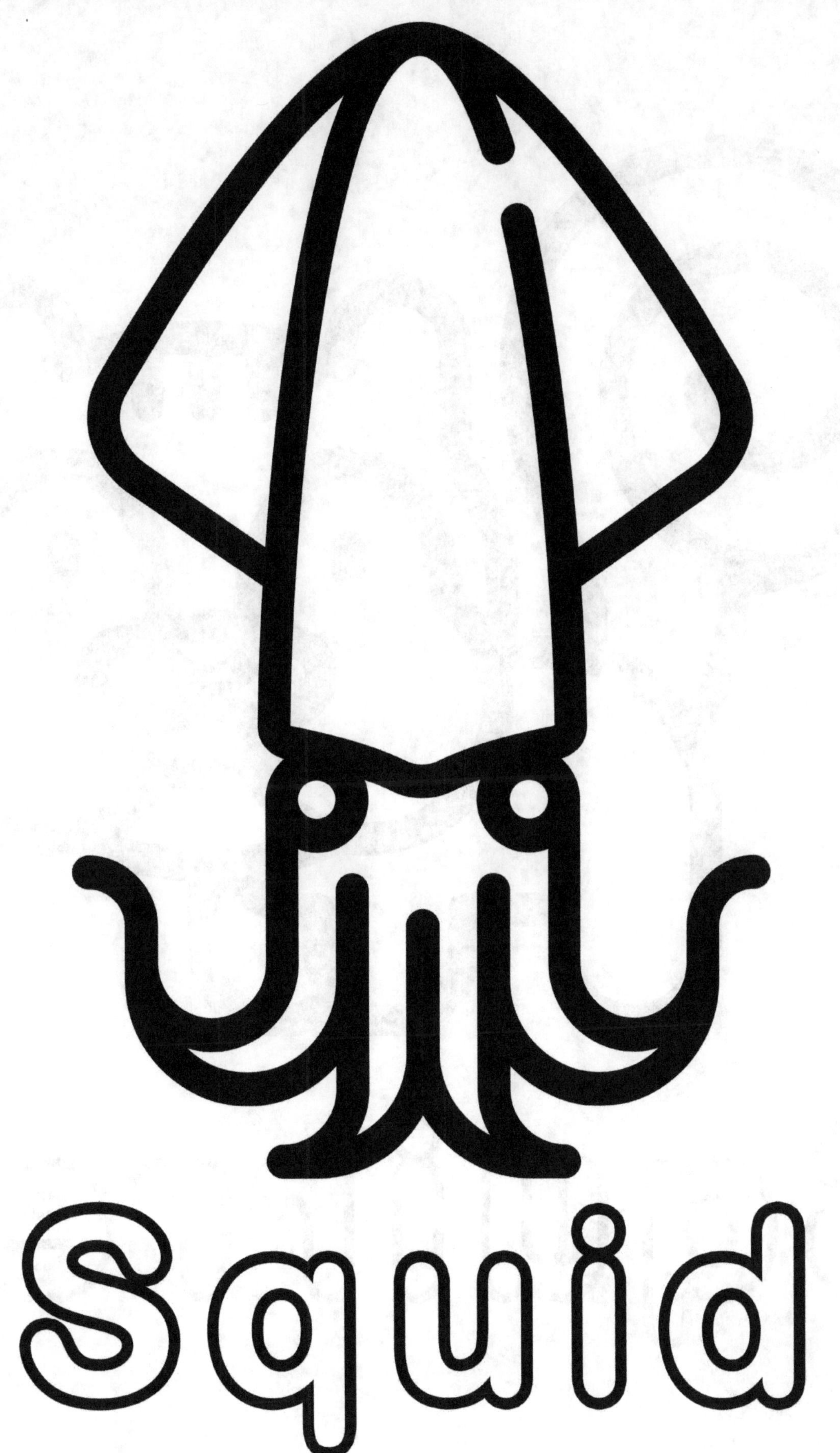


Squid

# Squirrel

Swan

# Swordfish

Tiger

Toucan

Turkey

# Turtle

Unicorn

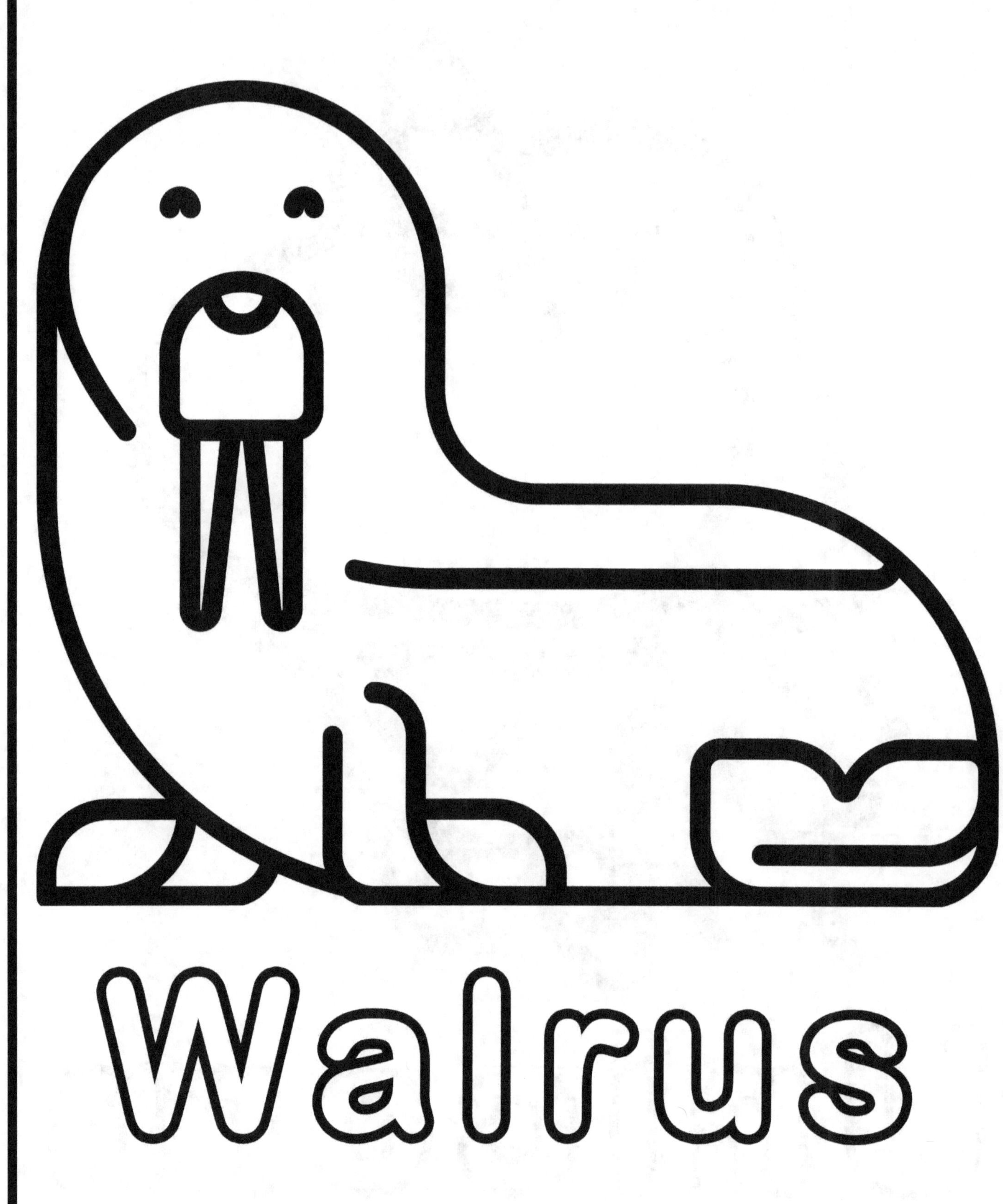

Walrus

Wasp

Whale

Wolf

Worm

# Zebra